This ACTIVITY BOOK
Belong to

____

____

____

1

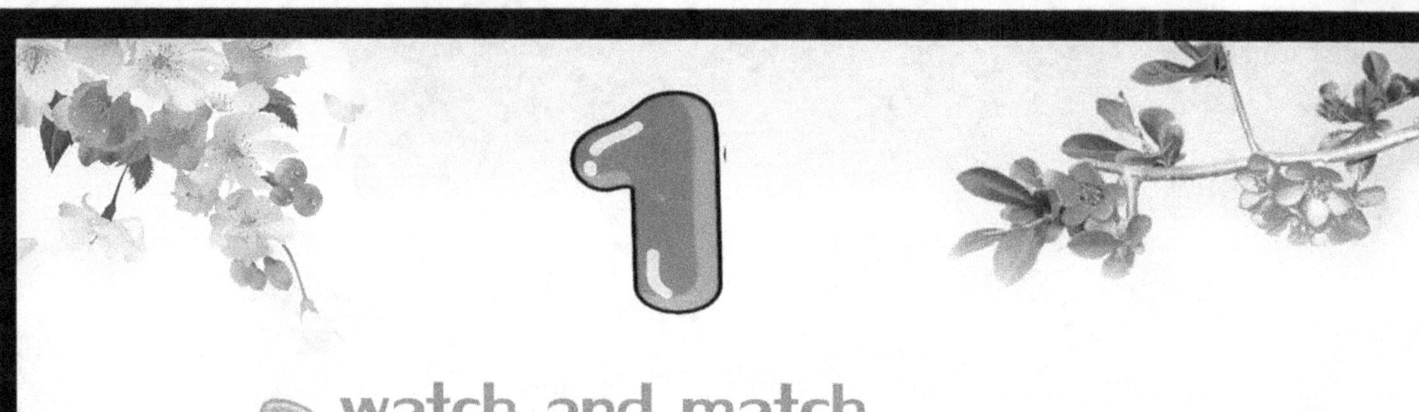

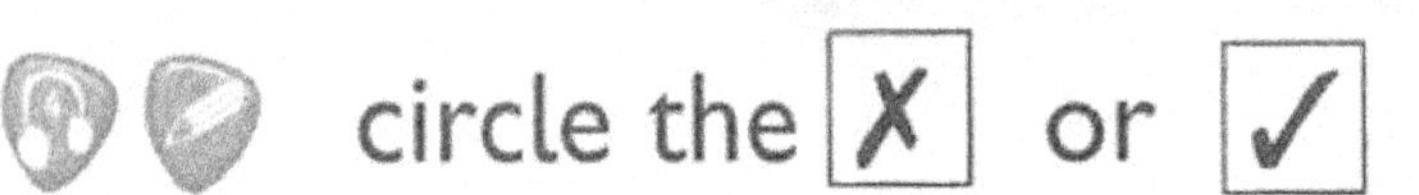

2

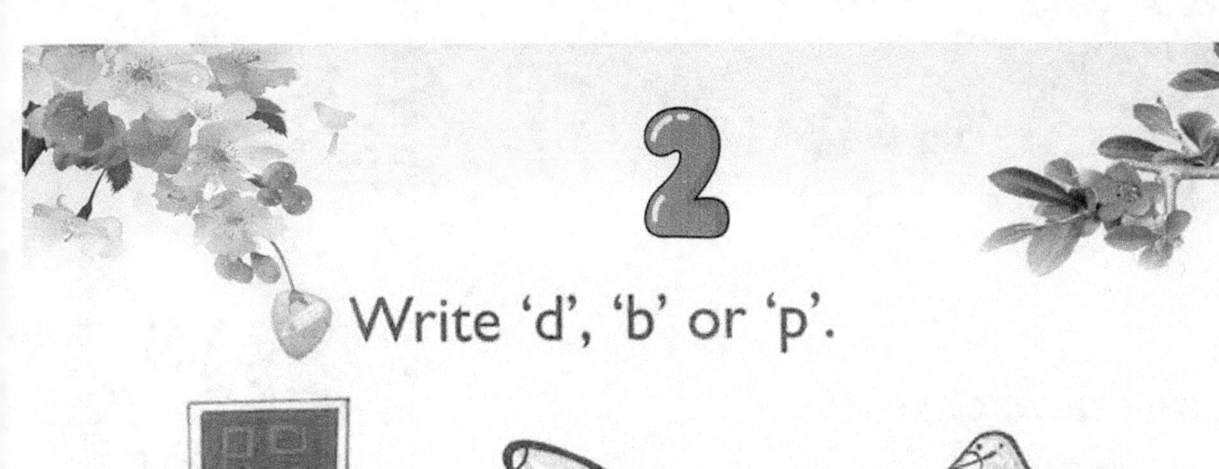

Write 'd', 'b' or 'p'.

Write the words.

| jacket | T-shirt | shoes | skirt | socks | trousers |

1 T-shirt

2

3

4

5

6

3

IMAGINE TRUE COLORS

4

Find and paste the correct pictures

Colour

FIND AND COLOR THE WORDS:

GAMES HAPPY
IOS MOBILE UNITY
ANDROID CAT BEE FUN

R A B O R C F A R Z G
G H S I S E U N E N U
N A E R O O N D H C E
F P M D R S C R U A O
T P Y E U K R O O T V
S Y Q S S U N I T Y B
E A G H S B P D Z E E
M O B I L E D O I E C
Q L L O R R J K B N F

6

Help mouse to find his way

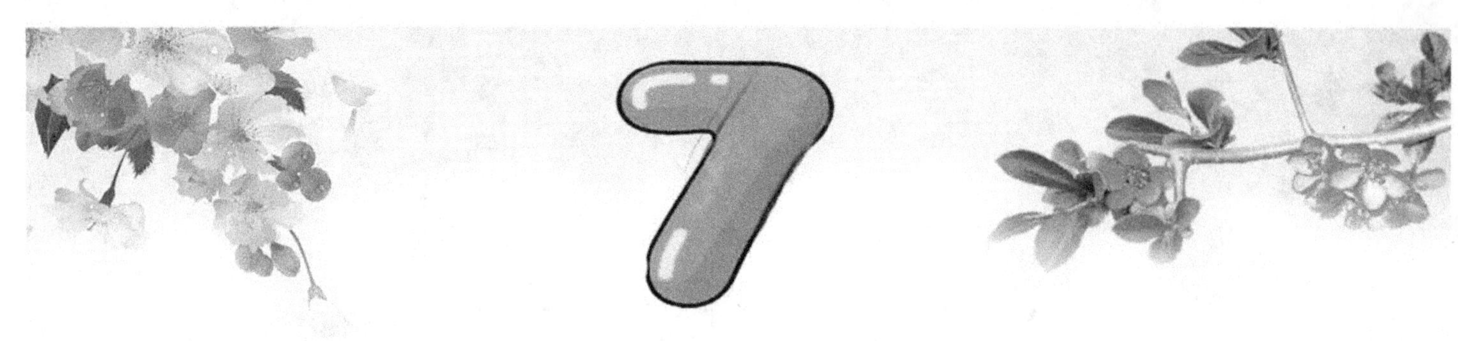

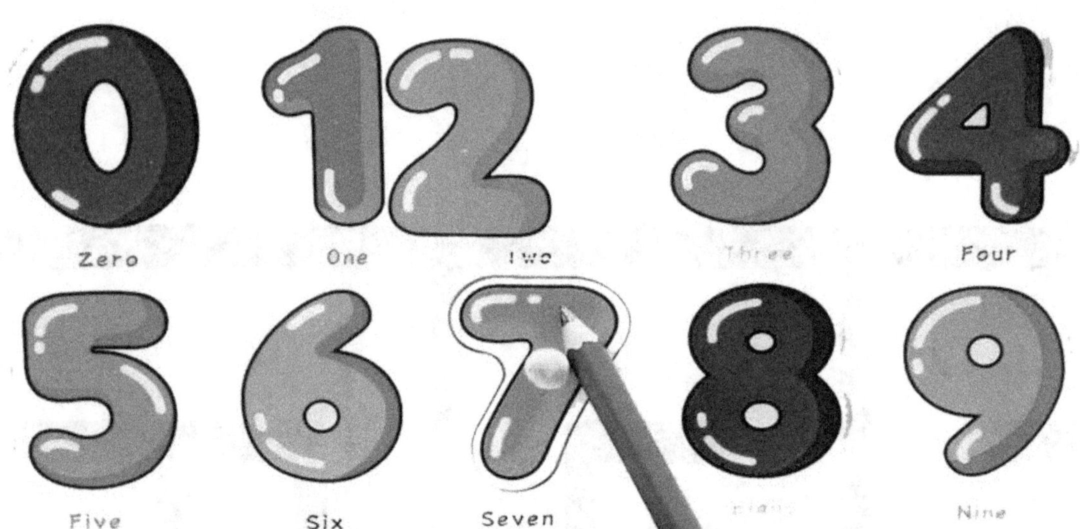

Zero
One
Two
Three
Four
Five
Six
Seven
Eight
Nine

show me how many

8

select true number by circle 

 (guitars)	1 8 7 6 5 4 10 9 2 3
(hats)	3 5 7 4 6 2 10 1 8 9
(bananas)	9 3 7 6 1 8 5 2 4 10
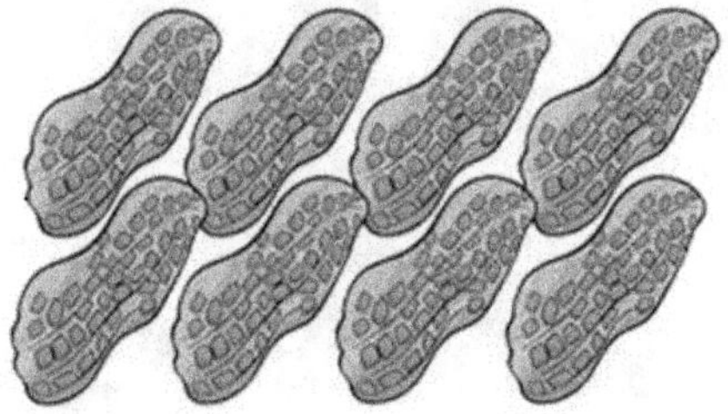 (peanuts)	8 1 6 3 9 7 2 10 5 4

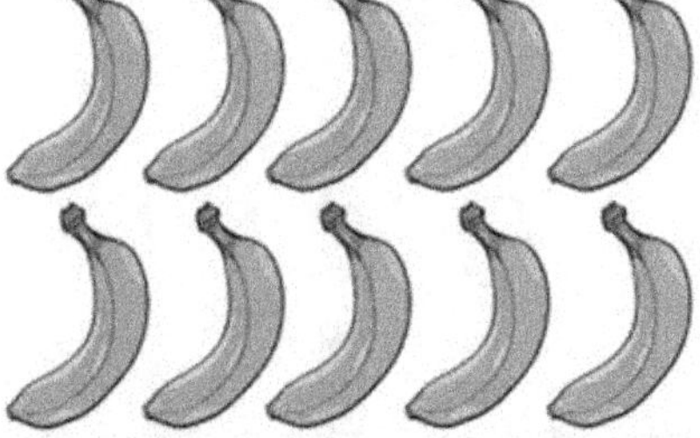

9

draw and colour.

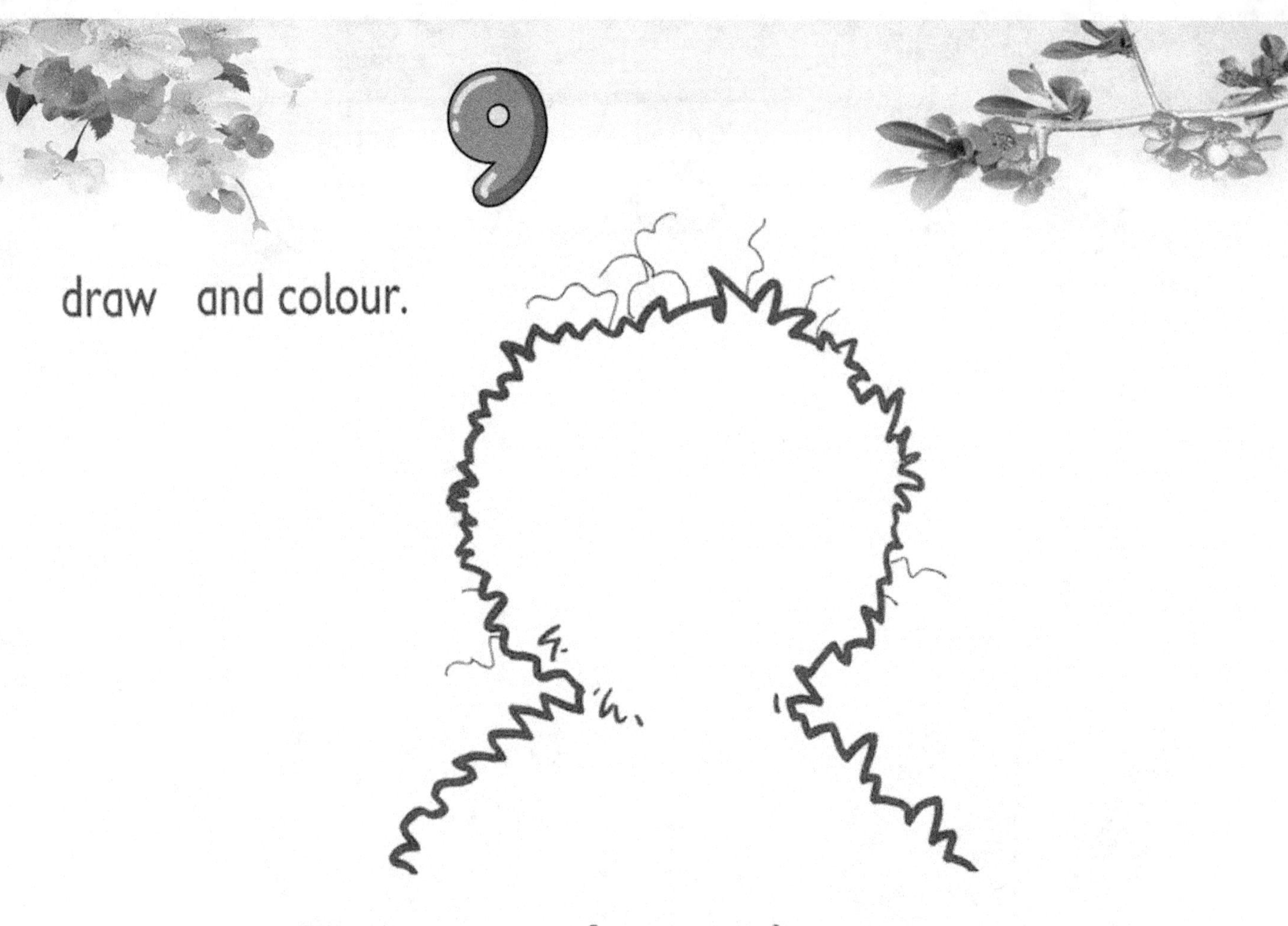

Draw your face and write.

I'm a star!

I've got .... eyes.

10

Write the words.

~~lorry~~	~~elephant~~	snake	helicopter	~~T-shirt~~	tiger
boat	trousers	plane	crocodile	skirt	jacket
shoes	motorbike	hippo	socks	giraffe	bus

lorry

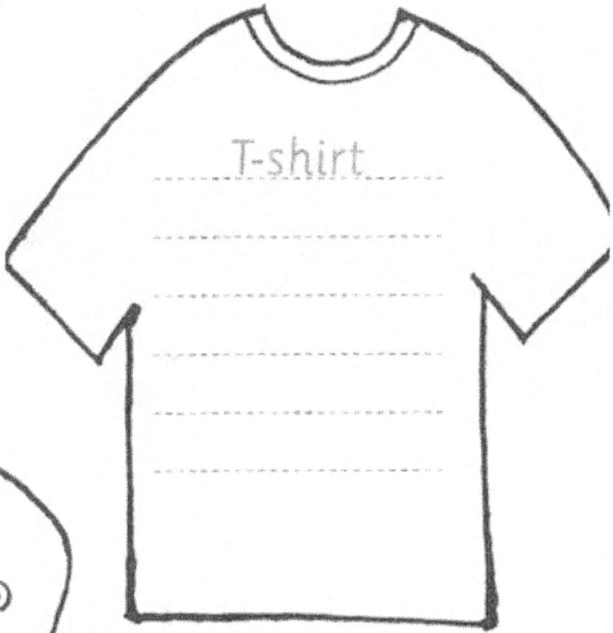

T-shirt

elephant

Count and colour.

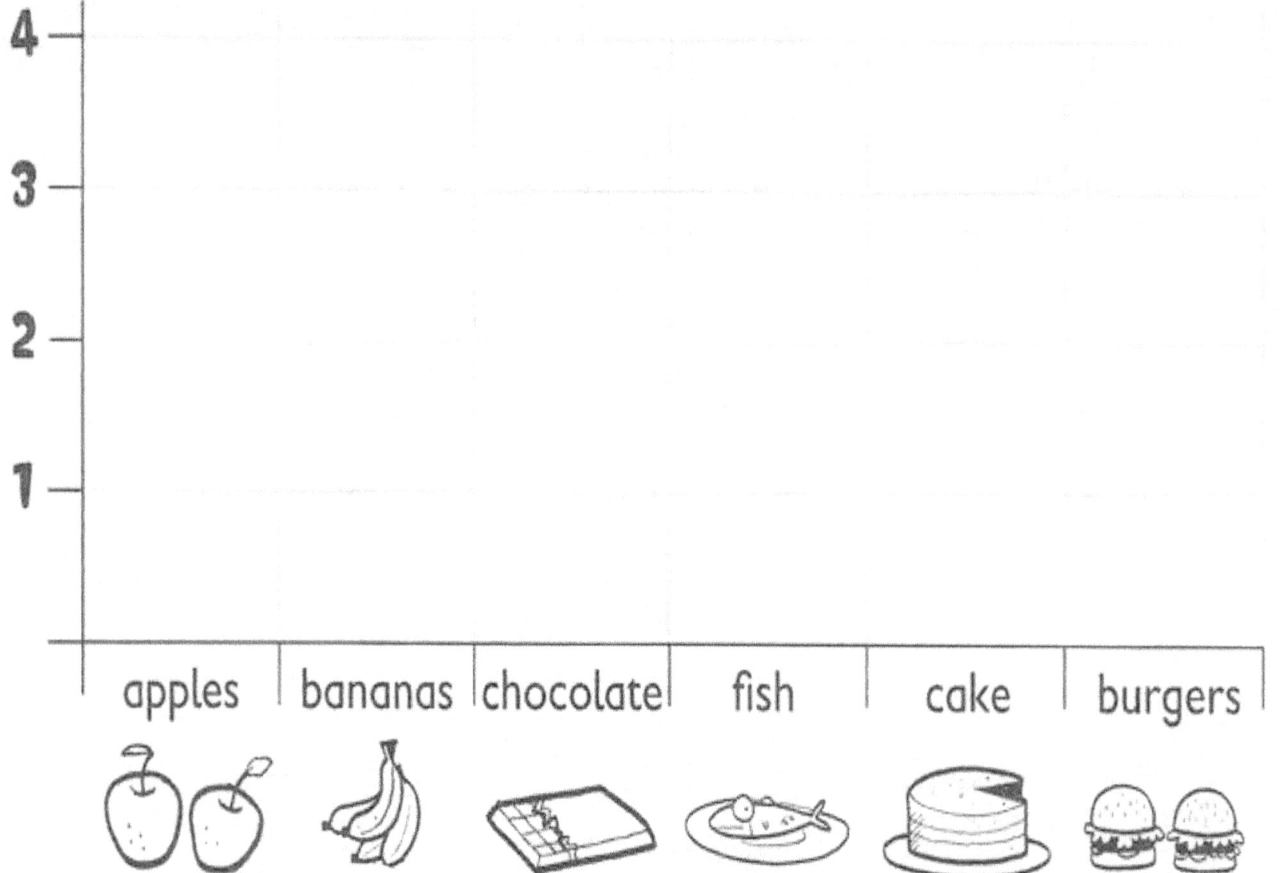

12

IMAGINE TRUE COLORS

Match and write the words.

| a bird | a cat | a dog | a fish | a horse | ~~a mouse~~ |

1

a mouse

2

3

4

5

6

14

Complete. Draw the food word.

1  2  3  4  5 

1    n   n
2    h   n
3   a   e
4 h   o   a
5 e c   m

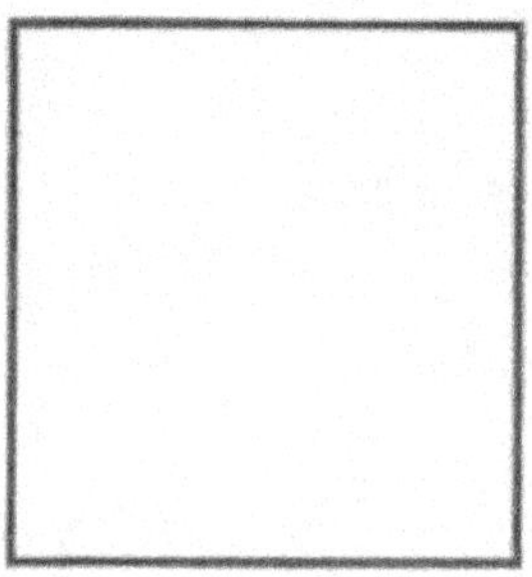

Write the words.

1    → cat

2    → ______

3 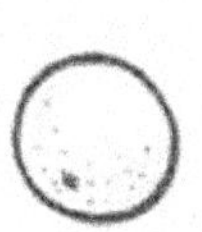   → ______

4    → ______

5    → ______

15

Colour the 't' words.

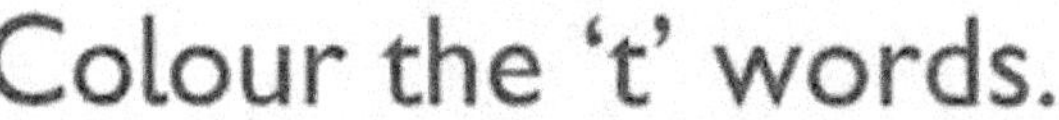

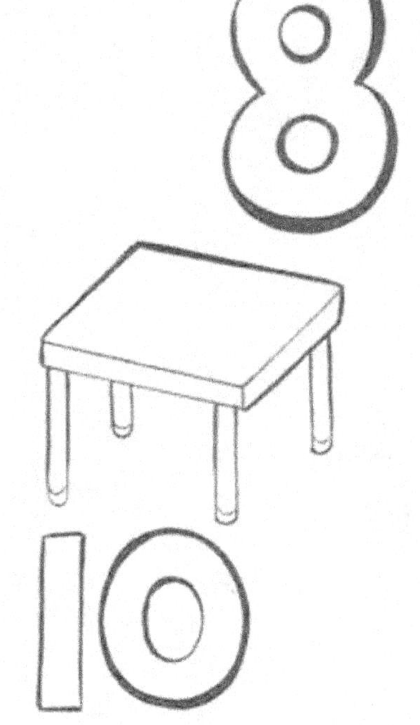

Tick four boxes. Play bingo.

Read and circle.

1. short / **(long)**
2. clean / dirty
3. small / big

4. short / long
5. big / small
6. clean / dirty

17

 Who is it? Match and answer.

 watch and colour.

Draw the animals. 18

5

6

7

8

9

10

Now tell your friend. Draw uour friend's animals.

5

6

7

8

9

10

Colour the clothes.

colour the star.

20

Look, write, read and draw.

a	b	c	d	e	f	g	h	i	j	k	l	m

n	o	p	q	r	s	t	u	v	w	x	y	z

1

s t o p

2

_ _ _ _ _ _

3

_ _ _ _ _ _

4

_ _ _ _ _ _ _ _ _ _ _ _

I Draw

21

I'm a star!

I'm ___patricia___ .

I'm ___five___ .

7

I'm a star!

I'm _______________ .

I'm _______________ .

22

 Follow the lines and write.

bedroom   living room   kitchen   hall

1 **2** **3** **4**

bedroom

Draw your house.

My house has got

🔍 Say the numbers. Look and answer.

Play the game.

24

picture dictionary

Can you say these words?

draw lines.

picture dictionary

Draw the pictures.

28

How many ?

1 + 2 + 3 + 1 = ☐

1 + 1 + 1 + 1 = ☐

1 + 2 + 3 + 2 = ☐

Draw the pictures.

❶	❷	❸
❹	❺	❻

Count and Color

HOW MANY ITEMS ARE IN EACH ROW?
WRITE THE NUMBER IN THE SQUARES.

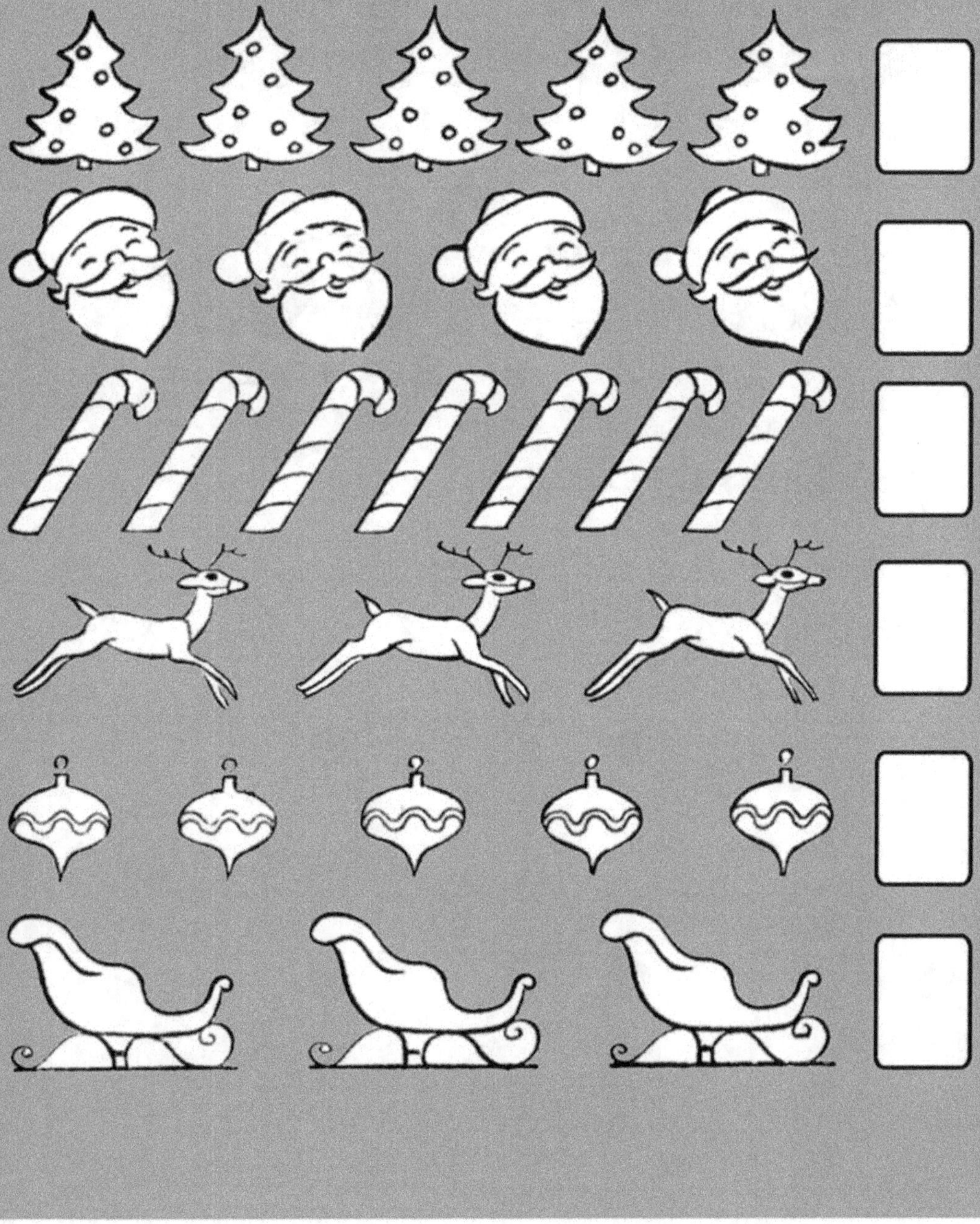

28

How many ?

1 + 2 + 3 + 1 = ☐

1 + 1 + 1 + 1 = ☐

1 + 2 + 3 + 2 = ☐

Draw the pictures.

❶	❷	❸
❹	❺	❻

29

How many ?

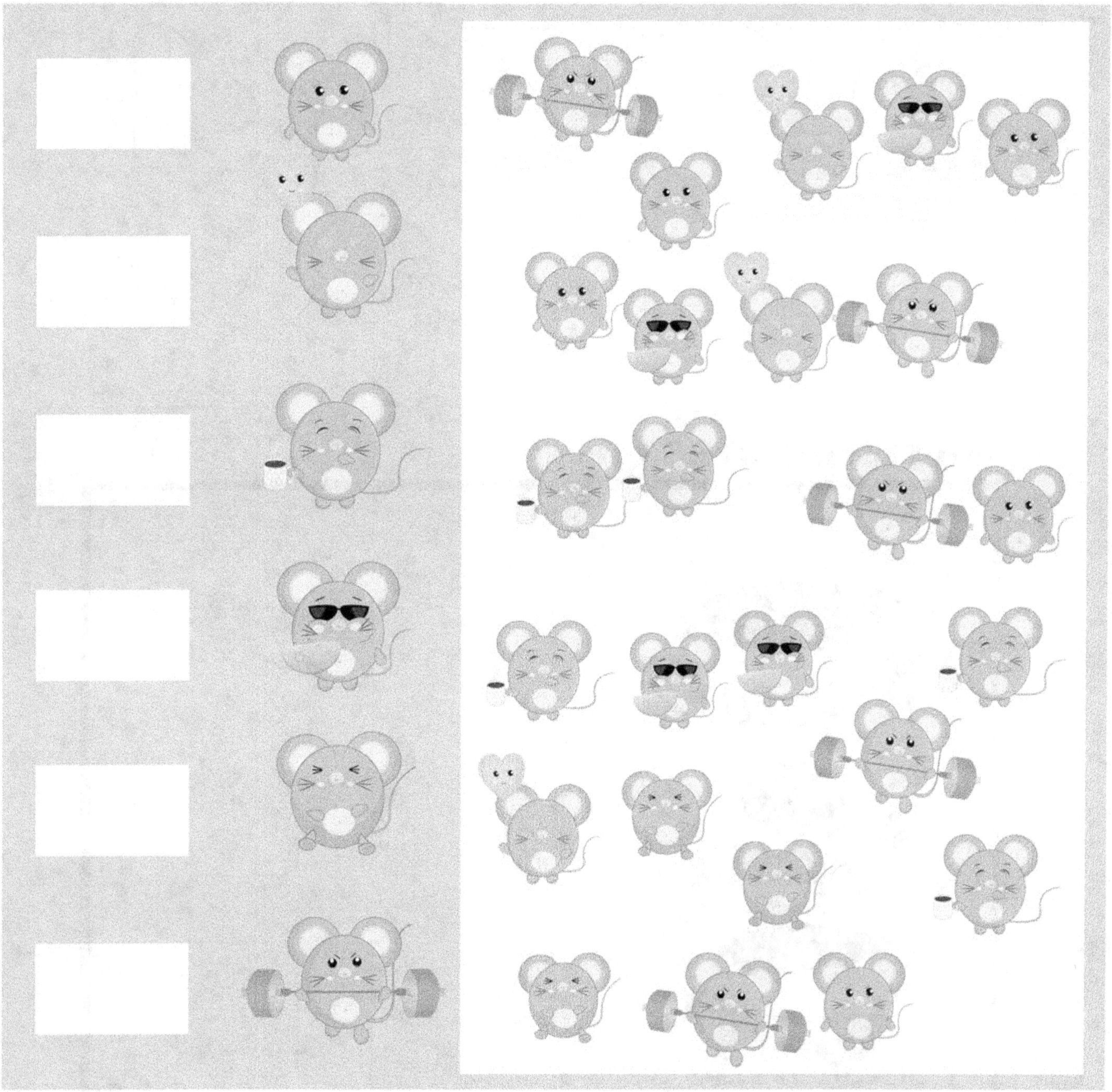

31

show me your birthday **year** by coloring the numbers

0 1 2 3 4
5 6 7 8 9

Find identical picturs:

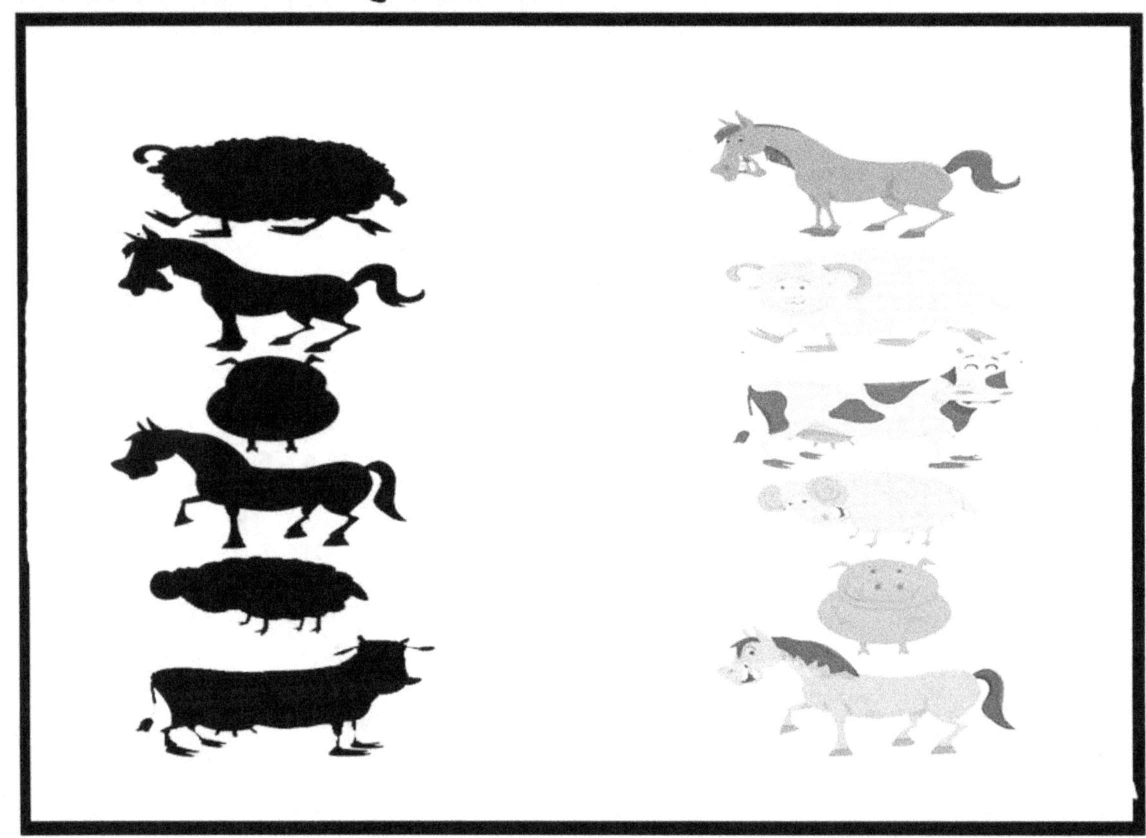

30

Draw the toys

 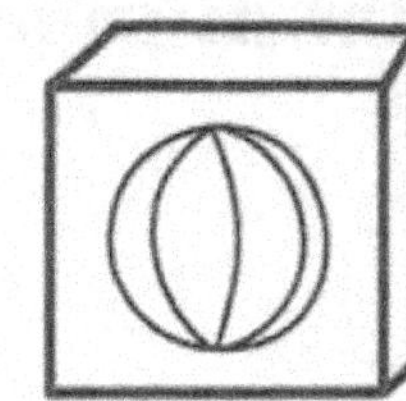   

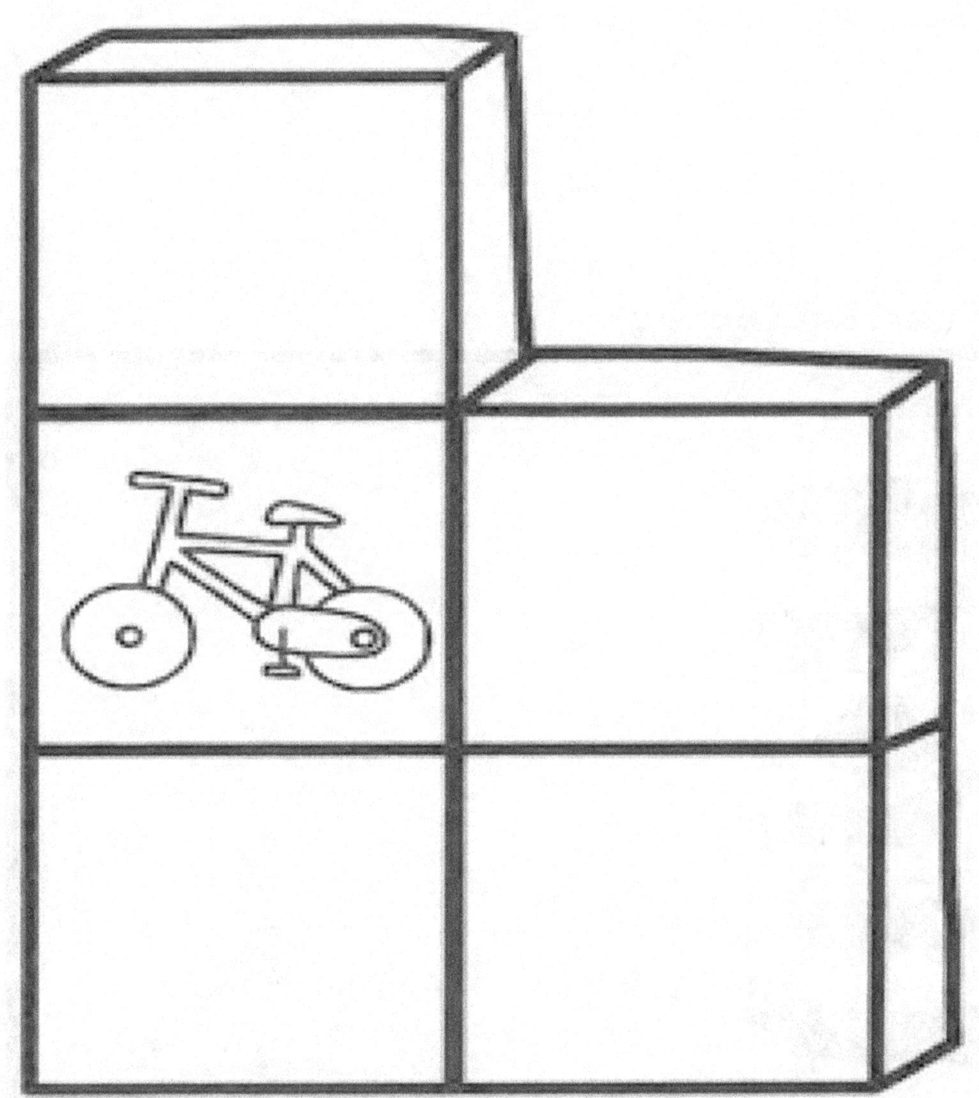

 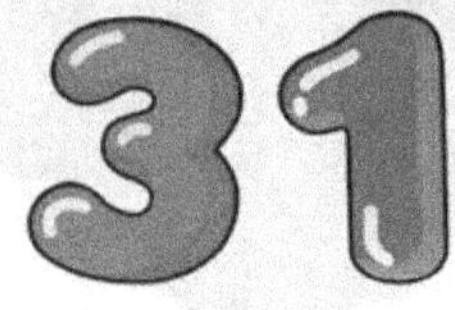 

31

show me your birthday year by coloring the numbers

Find identical picturs:

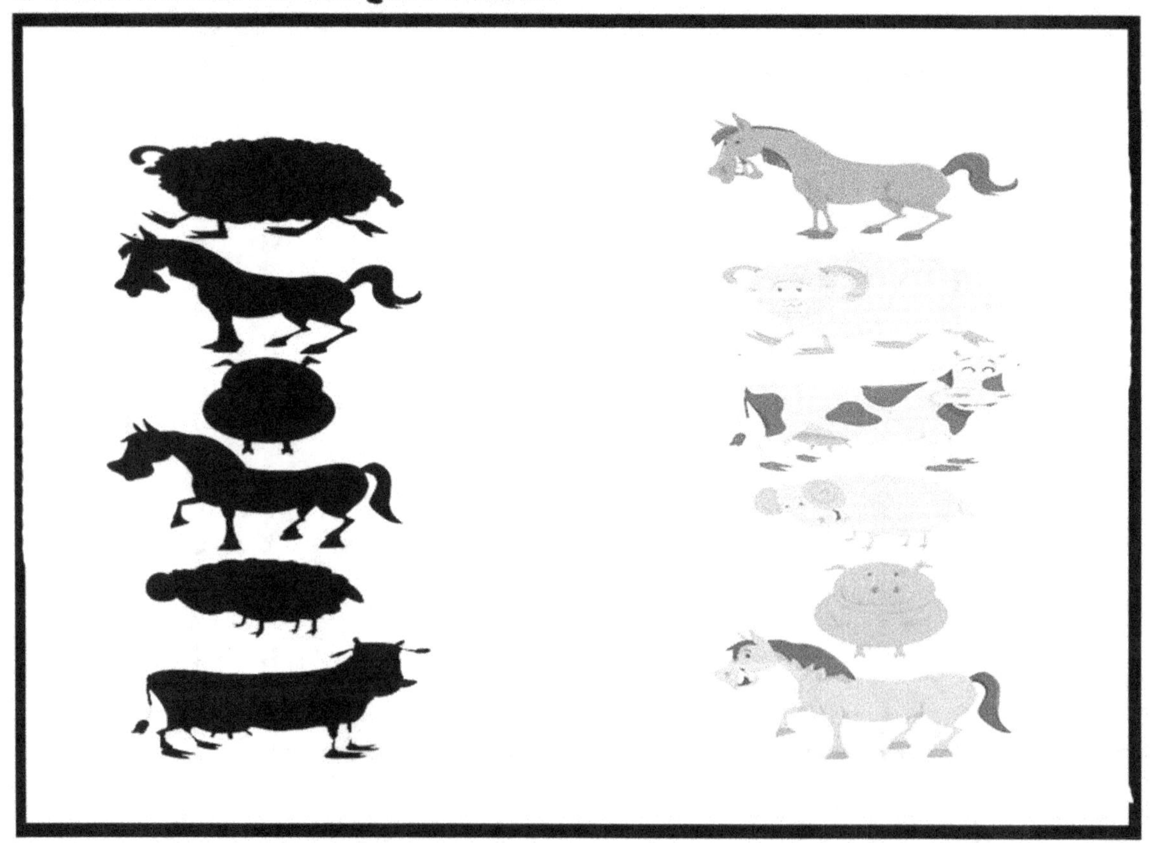

Imagine a princess in her true form

Try not to repeat the same color 3 times

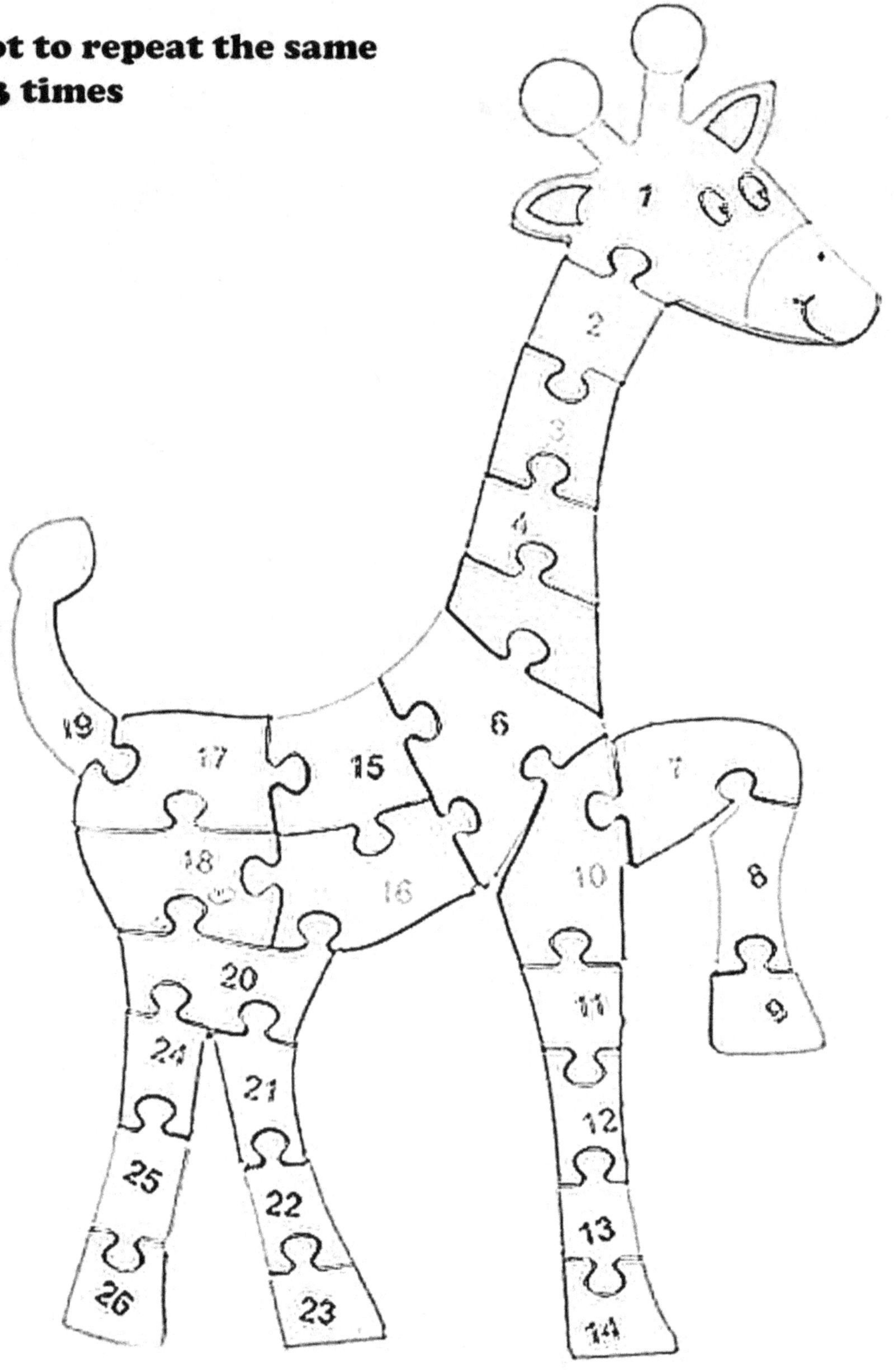

34

Imitate the colors of your cat
or your neighbor's cat

35

Bring life back to the forest and to King Simba

36

**IMAGINE TRUE COLORS

read and color

3 9 2 5
10 7 1

Play bingo.

38

IMAGINE TRUE COLORS

Drive each one to their favorite food with a different color/

Aladdin and the blue genie

41

word puzzle game

lacrosse

polo

G	L	K	Q	O	O	E	W	Y	O	H
N	J	A	J	M	Y	I	Q	O	K	J
I	Q	Y	C	X	B	Z	Q	G	J	I
F	G	A	D	R	G	N	I	M	M	I
R	B	K	E	F	O	Z	T	C	O	Q
U	O	I	K	R	D	S	P	F	Q	I
S	X	N	D	G	L	O	S	U	P	H
D	I	G	T	O	L	H	U	E	Z	G
N	N	X	N	O	Q	Y	S	V	I	Z
I	G	O	D	N	O	W	K	E	A	T
W	L	H	H	O	C	K	E	Y	T	P

boxing

kayaking

windsurfing

taekwondo

hockey

Thanks and Acknowledgements

The authors and publishers would like to thank the following consultants for their invaluable feedback:

We would also like to thank all the teachers who allowed us to observe their classes, and who gave up their invaluable time for interviews and focus groups.

The authors and publishers are grateful to the following illustrators:

The authors and publishers would like to thank the children

Made by:

Mr armoye sam
JAMAL MSS